Ken Urban

Sense of an Ending

Bloomsbury Methuen Drama
An imprint of Bloomsbury Publishing Plc

B L O O M S B U R Y
LONDON · NEW DELHI · NEW YORK · SYDNEY

Bloomsbury Methuen Drama
An imprint of Bloomsbury Publishing Plc

Imprint previously known as Methuen Drama

50 Bedford Square	1385 Broadway
London	New York
WC1B 3DP	NY 10018
UK	USA

www.bloomsbury.com

Bloomsbury is a registered trade mark of Bloomsbury Publishing Plc

© Ken Urban, 2015

British Library Cataloguing-in-Publication Data
A catalogue record for this book is available from the British Library.

ISBN: PB: 978-1-4742-4849-5
ePub: 978-1-4742-4851-8
ePDF: 978-1-4742-4850-1

Library of Congress Cataloging-in-Publication Data
A catalog record for this book is available from the Library of Congress.

Typeset by Mark Heslington Ltd, Scarborough, North Yorkshire

DEUS EX MACHINA
PRODUCTIONS

Sense of an Ending

Cast
(in order of appearance)

Sister Justina	Lynette Clarke
Sister Alice	Akiya Henry
Charles	Ben Onwukwe
Paul	Abubakar Salim
Dusabi	Kevin Golding

Creatives

Writer	Ken Urban
Director	Jonathan O'Boyle
Designer	Cecilia Carey
Lighting Designer	Joshua Pharo
Sound Designer	Max Perryment
Assistant Director	Hannah Jones
Assistant Designer	Harriet Bennett
Production Manager	James Ashby
Stage Manager	Rike Berg
Prosthetics	Carys Brown
Trailer	Zoya Films
Graphic Designer	Craig Slade
Production Photographer	Jack Sain
Marketing Assistant	Oliver Tobey
Producers	Jessica Campbell & Ramin Sabi for D.E.M. Productions

Cast

Lynette Clarke | Sister Justina

Stage credits include: *Boi Boi is Dead* (West Yorkshire Playhouse and Watford Palace), *The Crucible* (West Yorkshire Playhouse), *Horrible Histories* (Birmingham Stage Company), *The Bacchae* (National Theatre of Scotland), *The Crucible* (RSC), *To Kill a Mockingbird, Stepping Out, The Matchmaker, Treasure Island, Man of the Moment* (Festival Theatre, Pitlochry) *Stepping Out, The Wizard of Oz, Arabian Nights, Dick Whittington* (Everyman Theatre, Cheltenham), *Talking with Angels, Biff the Boxer* (Quicksilver Theatre), *Plague of Innocence* (Leicester Haymarket) and *Anasi* (Southwark Playhouse).

Television credits include: *Top Boy* (Channel 4), *Crimewatch Solved* (BBC) and *Harley Street* (ITV).

Akiya Henry | Sister Alice

Stage credits include: *A Midsummer Night's Dream, Words* (Bristol Old Vic), *Much Ado About Nothing, Henry V, Shakespeare in a Suitcase* (RSC New York), *Love Labour's Lost, Once in a Lifetime, Anything Goes, Coram Boy* (National Theatre) and *The Tempest, Hello Dolly, The Beggar's Opera* (Regent's Park Open Air Theatre).

Television credits include: *Silent Witness, Doctors, Little Britain, Casualty* (BBC).

Film credits include: *The Best Man, Calcium Kid* (Working Title Films).

Ben Onwukwe | Charles

Stage credits include: *Sunset Baby* (Gate Theatre), *Pandora's Box* (Arcola Theatre), *Man in the Middle* (Theatre503), *Macbeth* (Out of Joint), *High Life* (Hampstead Theatre), *Doctor of Honour* (Cheek by Jowl), *The Winter's Tale, Days of Significance, Pericles* (RSC), *A Family Business* (Oxford Playhouse), *The After Dinner Joke, The Making of Moo, Play without Repeats* (Orange Tree Theatre).

Television credits include: *Holby City* (BBC), *Coronation Street* (ITV), *The Bill* (Talkback Thames), *Law and Order* (NBC), *London's Burning* (ITV).

Radio credits include: *The No. 1 Ladies' Detective Agency* (BBC).

Abubakar Salim | Paul

Abu recently graduated from LAMDA (Genesis Foundation Scholar).

Stage credits include: *Prince of Denmark* (National Theatre), *Lift Off, Attempts on Her Life, Love and a Bottle, A Midsummer Nights Dream, Cymbeline, A Few Good Men* (LAMDA).

Television credits include: *Spotless* (CANAL+), *24: Live Another Day* (TCFTV) and *The Jury II* (ITV).

Kevin Golding | Dusabi

Stage credits include: *Play Mas* (Orange Tree Theatre), *Home Sweet Home* (Freedom Studios), *Otieno* (Southwark Playhouse), *Fan the Flame* (Theatre Royal Stratford East), *Children of the Crown, Mother Courage and her Children* (Nottingham Playhouse), *Othello* (White Bear Theatre), *Reality Chokes* (London Theatre Assembly) and *Macbeth* (Northcott Theatre).

Television credits include: *Silent Witness* (BBC), *House of Games* (Channel 4), *Footballers' Wives* (Shed Productions), *Dark Matters 2* (Wide-Eyed Entertainment) and *The Canterbury Tales* (BBC).

Film credits include: *It Never Sleeps* (Lost Eye), *The Fallen Word* (Celestial), *Counterfeit Butterfly* (IJE Films), *The Plague* (Armanda).

Short film credits include: *Terminally Happy* (Toybox/DUO), *Jasper* (Shereen Billings), *Turning Point* (Nu Skin).

Radio credits include: *Naija Bride* (BBC).

Ken Urban | Writer

Ken is a New York-based playwright. His plays have been produced across America.

Recent plays include: *A Future Perfect, The Awake, The Correspondent, The Female Terrorist Project, The Private Lives of Eskimos* and *The Happy Sad*. He has been awarded a Huntington Playwriting Fellowship, a Headlands Center for the Arts Residency, a Djerassi Artist Residency, the Dramatist Guild Fellowship, two MacDowell Colony Fellowships and a Residency at London's Donmar Warehouse. He wrote the screenplay for a feature film adaptation of his play *The Happy Sad*, which screened internationally. He is a Core Writer at the Playwright's Centre. His plays are published by Dramatists Play Service and Methuen.

Sense of an Ending won the Best New Play award at Williamstown Theatre Festival and receives its UK premiere at Theatre503.

www.kenurban.org

Jonathan O'Boyle | Director

Jonathan trained at the Central School of Speech and Drama and Birkbeck, University of London. He was the Resident Director at Sheffield Crucible and in 2014 he featured as one of the *Guardian*'s Rising Stage Stars.

Directing credits include: *The Surplus, All the Ways to Say Goodbye* (Young Vic), *The Verb, To Love, Made in Britain* (Old Red Lion), *Bash Latterday Plays* (Trafalgar Studios), *Water Under the Board* (Theatre503), *Last Online Today, Guinea Pigs* (Sheffield Crucible Studio) and *The Monster Bride* (Tristan Bates Theatre).

Associate Director credits include: *Mack and Mabel* (Chichester Festival Theatre), *Bull* (Young Vic/Sheffield Crucible) and *This is My Family* (Sheffield Lyceum/UK Tour).

Assistant Director credits include: *Amadeus* (Chichester Festival Theatre), *The Scottsboro Boys* (Young Vic), *Manon* (Royal Opera House), *My Fair Lady, The Village Bike* (Sheffield Crucible) and *Someone Who'll Watch Over Me* (Southwark Playhouse).

Cecilia Carey | Designer

Designer credits include: *The Surplus* (Young Vic), *Inside* (Latchmere Prison), *Pioneer* (Watford Palace Theatre and Touring: winner of 2014 Fringe First award), *Viral* (NYT Epic Stages at the Barbican), *The Imaginarium* (The Village Underground and Secret Productions), *The Last Days of Judas Iscariot* (Arts Ed), *Haining Dreaming* (Selkirk Estate), *The Inquiline* (The Yard), *The Pilgrim's Progress* (St James' Church), *A Hundred Shining Hearts* (Palace Theatre), *Lucy and The Hawk* (Northern Stage), *The Great Train Dance* (Severn Valley Railway), *The Red Helicopter* (Almeida Theatre).

Assistant/Associate Designer credits include: *On Off* (Aarhus Teater, Denmark), *The Closing Ceremony* (Olympics), *Batman* (World Tour), *Take That Tour* (UK Tour), *Kanye West Tour* (UK Tour), *OMG!* (The Place and Sadler's Wells).

www.ceciliacarey.com

Joshua Pharo | Lighting Designer

Joshua works as a Lighting and Projection Designer across theatre, dance, opera, music, film and art installation.

Credits include: *Unborn in America* (The Vault Festival), *The Mikvah Project* (Yard Theatre), *Amadis de Gaulle* (Bloomsbury Theatre), *Beckett Season* (Old Red Lion), *The Deluge* (UK Tour), *Usagi Yojimbo* (Southwark Playhouse), *A Streetcar Named Desire Parallel* (Young Vic), *Trace Elements* (UK Tour), *Werther* (Arcola Theatre), *Pioneer* (UK Tour), *I'd Rather Goya Robbed Me of My Sleep* (The Gate), *Thumbelina* (UK Tour), *No Place Like Home* (The Gate), *Pelleas et Melisande* (Arcola and Bury Court).

Video Design credits include: *Nicobobinus* (UK Tour), *Fox Symphony* (Camden People's Theatre), *The Hundred We Are* (Yard Theatre), *Brothers of Justice* (Camden People's Theatre).

Associate Video Designer credits include: *The Curious Incident of the Dog in the Night-Time* (Gielgud Theatre).

www.joshuapharo.com

Max Perryment | Sound Designer

Max is a composer, musician and sound designer living in London. He has composed music for a range of visual media, TV adverts, theatre and dance. Max is the resident composer for *Parrot in the Tank* and has an MA in Electroacoustic Composition from City University.

www.maxperryment.co.uk

Hannah Jones | Assistant Director

Hannah was Resident Assistant Director at the Finborough Theatre where she assisted on *Carthage, White Carnation, Fishskin Trousers, The Precariat* and a rehearsed reading of *The Pavilion*. Hannah is Company Director of Man In Rum Ltd and is producing a feature film, *A Smallholding*.

Director credits include: *Numb* (Baron's Court Theatre), *Cold Call* (Southwark Playhouse) and *Love Camp* (Park Theatre).

Assistant Director credits include: *Smallholding* (Soho Theatre) and *For a Look or a Touch* (King's Head Theatre).

Harriet Bennett | Assistant Designer

Harriet is currently studying for a BA in Costume Design at Wimbledon College of Art. She has worked as a Costume Assistant on *The Huntsman* (Universal Pictures Film), *The Review* (Mortimer Dramatic Society) and *Alice Through the Looking Glass* (The Iris Theatre).

James Ashby | Production Manager

James is training at East 15 Acting School, studying carpentry as his major.

Production Management credits include: *Donkey Heart* (Trafalgar Studios), *The Njogel Opera* (Tête à Tête Opera Festival) and Assistant Production Manager on *The Little Green Swallow* (The Peacock Theatre).

Rike Berg | Stage Manager

Rike graduated from the Bauhaus University, Weimar in Germany, and has worked on numerous productions in both Sweden and the UK. Since moving to London, Rike has worked for the Pleasance London and the Gate Theatre.

Credits as Stage Manager/Assistant Stage Manager include: *The Woman in Black* (Gothenburg English Studio Theatre and Sweden Tour), *Belongings* (GEST), *Into the Woods* (Stora Teatern, Gothenburg), *Grounded* (GEST) and *Upper Cut* (Southwark Playhouse).

Jessica Campbell & Ramin Sabi for Deus Ex Machina Productions | Producers

Deus Ex Machina Productions Ltd was set up by Ramin Sabi and Jessica Campbell to produce bold new theatre in London's Off West End. Through D.E.M. Ramin and Jessica have produced: *How I Learned to Drive* (Southwark Playhouse), the West End transfer of *Donkey Heart* (Trafalgar Studios), *Stink Foot* (The Yard Theatre), *Piranha Heights* (Old Red Lion) and *A Bright Room Called Day* (Southwark Playhouse). Their productions have received nine OffWestEnd award nominations. Ramin is Co-Producer for *Gypsy* in London's West End (Savoy Theatre) and Jessica is producing showcases of two new plays – *Four Play* and *Green Living* – for the Old Vic New Voices (Old Vic Theatre).

Thanks

This production would like to thank Dr Payam Akhavan, Sarah Arnold (at Press People), Azure Group, Micah Balfour, Annie Brewer and Jon Opie (at Jerwood Space), Dr Phil Clarke, Michael Davenport, Sue Emmas and Ben Cooper Melchiors (at the Young Vic), Gate Theatre, Franky Green, Steve Harper, Liam Harrison, Polly Ingham, Cornell S John, Jean Baptiste Kayigamba (translator), Neil Laidlaw, Alex Lowenstein, Michelle Mbau, Dr Linda Melvern, Okezie Morro, Sandra Reid, Royal Victoria Hall Foundation, Patrice Shema, Toby Simpson (at Wiener Library), Cleo Sylvestre, Paul Robinson, Andrew Wildgoose, James Wizeye (at the Rwandan High Commission), Lisa Yacoub (Bridge of Hope).

Playwright's Thanks

Ken would like to thank all of the directors and actors who have worked on this play, especially Jonathan O'Boyle. My thanks to the MacDowell Colony for the time and space to finish crucial revisions. A big thanks to the people who believed in this play, even when I didn't. You know who you are.

The text went to press before the end of rehearsals and so may differ slightly from the play as performed.

THEATRE503

Theatre503 is the award-winning home of groundbreaking plays.

Led by Artistic Director Paul Robinson, Theatre503 is a flagship fringe venue committed to producing new work that is game-changing, relevant, surprising, mischievous, visually thrilling and theatrical. Our theatre is one of London's few destinations for new writing and we offer more opportunities to new writers than any other theatre in the country.

THEATRE503 TEAM

Artistic Director – Paul Robinson

Executive Director – Jeremy Woodhouse

Producer and Head of Marketing – Polly Ingham

Associate Artistic Director – Lisa Cagnacci

Office Manager – Emily Hubert

Literary Manager – Steve Harper

Literary Coordinators – Lauretta Barrow, Tom Latter

Resident Assistant Producers – Franky Green, Liam Harrison

Volunteer Coordinators – Serafina Cusack, Simon Mander

'Young Creative Leaders' Project Manager – Louise Abbots

Senior Readers – Kate Brower, Karis Halsall, Clare O'Hara, Jimmy Osbourne, Imogen Sarre

Associate Directors – Gemma Fairlie, Tom Littler

THEATRE503 BOARD

And we couldn't do what we do without out brilliant volunteers:

Annabel Pemberton, Nuno Faisca, Rosie Akerman, Diyan Zora, Tobias Chapple, Joseph Ackerman, Alexandra Coyne, Anuska Zaremba-Pike, Cecilia Segar, Valeria Bello, Larner Taylor, Damian Robertson, Jumoke, Valeria Carboni, Mike Bale, Serafina Cusack, Lousie Fairbrother, Caroline Jowett, Jim Mannering, Oluwafuntu Ojumu, Imogen Robertson, Chidimma Chukwu, Jill Segal, Elena Valentine, Tess Hardy, Kenneth Hawes, Anna Gorajek, Maya Kirtley.

Theatre503 is supported by:

Angela Hyde-Courtney and the Audience Club, Kay Ellen Consolver, Cas Donald, Edna Kissman, Eileen Glynn, Deborah Shaw and Steve Marqhardt, Marisa Drew, Jerwood/Posonby, Andrew and Julia Johnson, Georgia Oetker, Stuart Mullins, Michael Morfey, Geraldine Sharpe-Newton, Penny Egan, Liz Padmore, Bernice Chitnis, Lisa Forrell, Abigail Thaw, Charlotte Westenra, Frankie Sangwin, Mike and Hilary Tyler, Sue and Keith Hamilton, Sandra Chalmers, David Chapman and Judy Molloy, Georgie Grant Haworth, Amy Rotherham, Kate Beswick, Craig Simpson, Jason Meiniger, Yve Newbold, Philip and Chris Carne, Juliana Breitenbach.

Theatre503, 503 Battersea Park Rd, London, SW11 3BW

020 7978 7040 | www.theatre503.com

Shine a light on Theatre503

Theatre503 receives no public subsidy as a venue and we cannot survive without the transformative support of our friends. For as little as £23 a year you can help us remain 'Arguably the most important theatre in Britain today' (*Guardian*).

Becoming a Friend of Theatre503 is simple.

Annual Support donations are invited in five tiers:

Footlight – £23

- Priority notice of productions and events
- Priority booking for all productions
- Special ticket offers
- E-mail bulletins

Spotlight – £53

As Footlight plus

- Access to sold-out shows
- Credit in the theatre foyer, play texts, and on the website

Limelight – £173

As Spotlight plus

- Two complimentary tickets to Theatre503's hottest new play each year
- Complimentary tickets to play readings and other one-off supporter events
- Free programmes
- Ticket exchange service for pre-booked tickets (with 24 hours' notice)

Highlight – £503

As Limelight plus

- Two complimentary tickets for each Theatre503 in-house production
- Opportunities to attend rehearsals
- Invitation to annual high-level supporters' party hosted by the Artistic Director

Starlight – £1,003

A bespoke package enables our Starlight to engage with Theatre503's work as they wish. This can include bespoke entertaining opportunities at the theatre, invitations to attend supper parties with the Artistic Director, or closer engagement with playwrights and the artistic team. Starlights can also choose a strand of Theatre503's work to support, for example a particular production, funding Theatre503 writing programmes or work in the local community. Please visit our website *theatre503.com* for details on specific appeals also.

One-off donations also make an enormous difference to the way Theatre503 is able to operate. Whether you are able to give £10 or £1,000 your gift will help us continue to create work of award-winning standard.

To become a member or make a one-off donation e-mail your interest to: *info@theatre503.com*, or by post to: Theatre503, The Latchmere, 503 Battersea Park Road, London, SW11 3BW.

Alternatively visit our website *theatre503.com* or ring 020 7978 7040 to sign up for membership directly.

If you are a UK taxpayer and able to make a gift aid donation please let us know as we receive 25p per pound more on top of your donation in government grant.

Sense of an Ending

For Matthew

Characters

Charles, *thirties, an African-American journalist from New York*
Paul, *twenties, a Tutsi corporal in the Rwandan Patriotic Front*
Sister Justina, *Bernadette, forties, a Catholic nun of the Benedictine order, Hutu*
Sister Alice, *Consolata, twenties, a Catholic nun of the Benedictine order, Hutu*
Dusabi, *forties, Tutsi*

The play is set in the city of Kigali in Rwanda, a country in central east Africa. It takes place over Easter weekend, 31 March–4 April 1999.

All punctuation and spacing is intentional and gives a sense of the line's delivery.

The N dash (–) at the end of the line indicates an interruption.

A slash (/) indicates that the following lines begin to overlap at that point.

When set aside as a line, an [. . .] is a pregnant pause, a moment when the character gets to the next place. It can be filled with sound or silence.

A shift is when time or location changes. They should be seamless, actor-driven events supported by sound and lights.

The native language of Rwanda is Kinyarwanda. Save for Charles, all of the characters speak English with a French-African accent.

While the play is based on the facts of the genocide, it is a work of fiction.

Decimation means the killing of every tenth person in a population, and in the spring and early summer of 1994, a program of massacres decimated the Republic of Rwanda. Although the killing was low-tech – performed largely by machete – it was carried out at dazzling speed: of an original population of about seven and a half million, at least eight hundred thousand were killed in just a hundred days. Rwandans often speak of a million deaths, and they may be right.

– Philip Gourevitch

We Wish to Inform You that Tomorrow We Will be Killed with Our Families

There is the question of our growing suspicions of fictions in general. But it seems that we still need them.

– Frank Kermode

The Sense of an Ending

Day One

Sisters Justina and Alice (*singing*)
> *Jesus loves me*
> *This I know*
> *Because the Bible tells me so*
> *Little ones to Him belong*
> *For they are weak*
> *But He is Strong*
>
> *Yes, Jesus Loves Me*
> *Yes, Jesus Loves Me*
> *Yes, Jesus Loves Me*
> *The Bible tells me so –*

Shift.

Charles (*into his recorder*)   Wednesday, March 31st, 1999. The guide the government assigned to me was supposed to take me directly to the jail. He stops at the church where the nuns lived and he shoots –

Gunshot. Shift. The yard in front of the church.

Paul   Got him.

Charles   This isn't the jail.

Paul   This is the church.

Charles   What did you shoot? Is that a –?

Paul   Dog.

Charles   Why would you do that? He wasn't doing anything.

Paul   Habit.

Charles   You make it a habit to shoot dogs?

Paul   The first few days we entered Kigali, we'd see them. Traveling in packs. Feeding on corpses. Shot one my first night, had a woman's thigh in his mouth.

Charles   Saw that in Serbia. Cats though.

Paul   Could never shoot a cat. I have a cat. Juliet. I have many cats. Ever since I was a boy. All called Juliet.

Charles   Really? You don't strike me as a cat person.

Paul   What is a cat person?

Charles   Paul and his pussy cats.

Paul   You teasing me?

Charles *laughs.*

Paul *cocks his rifle.*

Paul   You tease me.

Charles   We need to go to the jail now.

Paul *observes* **Charles** *for a moment.* **Paul** *takes out a canteen and offers it to* **Charles**.

Paul   Water, Charles?

Charles   Thanks.

Charles *takes a swig.*

Charles (*coughs*)   That isn't water.

Paul (*smiles*)   Strong, yes?

Charles   Not bad.

Charles *takes a small swig and gives the canteen back.* **Paul** *takes a bigger swig.*

Paul   I take you inside the church now. The bodies, we left as we found them. It is a way to remember those who died here.

Charles   My story is the nuns.

Paul   This is where the nuns lived.

Charles   The nuns haven't lived here in half a decade. The jail, Paul. They're waiting for me.

Paul   It isn't far. Our roads are good. It won't be long.

Charles   This is a big story. Everyone in the world is watching. It's gonna be a landmark trial. A Belgian court trying Rwandans for events during the genocide.

Paul   These nuns should face trial here. What do Belgians know of Rwanda?

Charles   When the Rwanda Patriotic Front, when your army entered Rwanda five years ago, you stopped the killings, restored peace. There was a lot of international support for you and the government you formed. But now? The RPF, how you look in the eyes of the world, it's not too good. We've reported on your treatment of prisoners. Denying them basic rights, convictions without trials –

Paul   And what of the crimes of these prisoners?

Charles   Alleged crimes. No one's been convicted. I've come here to speak with the nuns, Paul. To hear their story, objectively. Without prejudice.

Paul   You like these nuns?

Charles   It isn't about that.

Paul   You worry that seeing inside the church will prejudice you against the nuns?

Charles   My assignment is waiting for me at the jail.

Paul   You're scared.

Charles   There isn't a famine, war zone, atrocity I haven't seen.

Paul   You've never seen anything like what's behind this door.

Charles   I can imagine –

Paul   No, you can't.

Pause.

Charles   You born here, in Kigali?

Paul   My family, they sent me away to Uganda when I was a kid. They stayed.

Charles   You joined the RPF, came back?

Paul   This is where I must be.

Charles   And your family? Are they Tutsi?

Paul   They were Rwandan.

Charles (*understanding what* **Paul** *is saying*)   I'm sorry for your loss.

Paul   We go inside the church now.

Charles   No.

Paul   All the same. Americans talk and never act.

Charles   Get me to the jail before lunchtime, I promise I'll come back before I go. Now, Paul, the jail, understand?

Shift. An interrogation room at a jail in Kigali.

Sister Justina   We do not think the lawyers have taken the time to learn the truth. There are many lies spoken about us.

Charles   *The Times* has been following events in Rwanda since the violence five years ago. But your story, it's a story that hasn't been told.

Sister Alice   Our story will be known?

Charles   *The New York Times*, it's read the world over.

Sister Justina   We speak only to you, to our lawyers in Belgium.

Charles   I am the only reporter you speak to. Understood? That's the agreement.

Sister Justina   Yes.

Charles *takes out a Dictaphone.*

Sister Alice   He will record this? You did not say he would /
record this –

Sister Justina   Consolata, please.

It is fine, Charles, to record what we say.

Charles   My guide Paul, he got, lost. We don't have much
time. Can we begin?

Sister Justina   Easter, this weekend.

Charles   Yes.

Sister Alice   You a Catholic?

Charles   I believe in goodness, Sisters.

Charles *switches on the recorder.*

Charles   Wednesday, March 31st, 1999. Kigali Central
Prison.

Please speak clearly into the recorder. State your names and
the crimes with which you are charged.

Sister Alice   Consolata. Sister Alice.

Sister Justina   Sister Justina. Bernadette.

Charles   And the charges you face?

Sister Justina   The court charges that we were complicit.
With crimes against humanity.

Charles   They also charge you with homicide.

Sister Justina   Yes.

Pause.

Charles   Tell me about your life at the parish, Sisters.

Sister Justina   Our life is the church.

Sister Alice   We wake up. After morning mass, cook
breakfast for Father Neromba and the men who care for
the grounds.

Sister Justina   Afternoons are spent with the children.

Sister Alice   Evening prayers. Supper.

Sister Justina   On Sunday –

Sister Alice   Sundays, large breakfast with many visitors, followed by mass, in the evening –

Sister Justina   Cooking, washing up, mending of clothes –

Sister Alice   That is our life.

Sister Justina   I remember the day Sister Alice joined us.

Sister Alice   Never been so far from my family before. Bernadette took care of me. She takes care of me still.

Sister Justina   Sister Alice was just a girl when she arrived at the parish.

Charles   Like a mother and daughter.

Sister Justina   Yes, perhaps.

Charles   How did you find out President Habyrarimana had been killed?

Silence.

Charles   Please. Walk me through the events of that day.

Sister Justina   It is a long time ago.

Charles   Yes, five years.

Sister Justina   The President. We are told his plane is shot down and all aboard perish. That is all we know.

Charles   And you, Sister Alice, what do you remember about that day?

Sister Alice   It is strange to say. But that was a happy time for us at the parish. Before all the trouble. I tell you, you think I am a silly nun.

Charles   Please.

Sister Alice   There was a miracle. The look in Father Neromba's eyes after she came to him. The Blessed Mother.

Sister Justina   Mary, the Mother of Jesus.

Sister Alice   Such joy. She spoke to Father on his morning walk / telling him –

Sister Justina   Sister Alice, the reporter did not travel all this way to hear us speak of miracles.

Charles   The Virgin Mary visited Father Neromba. What did she say to him?

Sister Alice   The Virgin Mother tells / Father that –

Sister Justina   Father, he does not say.

Charles *notices the tension.*

Charles (*to* **Sister Alice**)   Sister, you were going to say . . .?

Sister Alice (*smiles*)   No, nothing.

Charles   Let me make sure I understand. The day of the miracle is also the day the President's plane is shot down.

Sister Justina   A man from town, Seth, he comes and tells us that night. The RPF. The Tutsi rebels, they shoot down the President's plane.

Charles   You are told the RPF kill President Habyrarimana?

Sister Justina   RPF is not innocent. They are soldiers. They invade our country.

Charles   The President was ready to sign a peace accord with the Rebel Army. These soldiers are Rwandan, forced out of their country by Habyrarimana's government.

Sister Alice   They kill people. The RPF.

Sister Justina   Charles, we do not question what we are told. We trust God watches over us and will keep us safe. We are Catholics.

Sister Alice (*suddenly stern*)   We are Hutus.

Sister Justina *notices the change in* **Charles***'s expression.*

Sister Justina   She does not mean that in the way you think.

Sister Alice   I mean only to say: We are Catholics. We are Hutu.

Charles   Tutsi. Hutu. I'm not from here. I can't tell the difference.

Sister Justina   If you were from here, you would know.

Sister Alice   We only want to return to our life in the church, Charles. The trouble begins and they take us to live in the hills. We live a quiet life far from the city for many years, hoping one day to return. Then one day RPF soldiers come, they arrest us for crimes we were not even present for. Made to live in this horrible prison, so many people, and the filth. Not fit for people, but animals. Every day I pray, I pray we can return to our parish.

Sister Justina *takes* **Sister Alice***'s hand.*

Sister Justina   We will, Consolata, we will.

Charles   Look, here are the facts. Five years ago, President Habyarimana's plane is shot down, killing him and everyone else onboard. It's unclear, even now, who's responsible. Immediately following the President's death, the Hutu extremists, who opposed the peace accord, they take control of the government. The curfew starts, roadblocks go up. The Hutu militias, men, boys, women even, armed with machetes, guns, pipes, begin to kill Tutsis. The killings continue for a hundred days until the RPF enter the country and return order. Eight hundred thousand Tutsi men, women and children are dead.

Sister Justina   We know this, Charles.

Charles   I wasn't here. My readers weren't here. The judge, your lawyers, the Belgian citizens who'll sit on your jury, none of them were here. But you were. You are the only two people who can speak about what happened at your church.

A bell rings somewhere in the prison.

Sister Justina   The guard will be on his way to take us to supper.

Charles   But we've only started.

Sister Justina   We have no say over such things.

Charles   Then we resume tomorrow.

Sister Justina   Yes. Tomorrow.

Charles   I will speak with you first, Sister Justina. Then Sister Alice.

Sister Justina   There was nothing in the agreement about / speaking to you separately –

Charles   I will speak with each of you separately.

Sister Justina   I am not sure that is best.

Charles   Let me speak bluntly, Sisters. Things don't look good for you. But you're not being tried here, in Rwanda, but in a Belgian court, in front of the world. That's an opportunity.

Sister Justina   You think we do not / know this –?

Sister Alice   Do you think we are innocent, Charles?

Charles   If my story can show the correct facts, if it becomes clear that the RPF is lying about your involvement in the massacre, that's a headline that will be talked about. If doubts were cast on the RPF's case, it could change the outcome of your trial. But this only happens if you talk to me.

Sister Justina   That is good for you, a big story.

Charles   It's good for all three of us.

Sister Alice *is unsteady.*

Sister Alice   Bernadette, I am unwell –

Shift. A hotel bar in Kigali.

Paul   One of them fainted?

Charles   Younger one.

Paul   She is good actress.

Charles   Is that what you think? You didn't see her.

Paul   Have another beer.

Charles   I had enough. I need sleep.

Paul   You drink our beer, you'll sleep well tonight.

Charles   Been a couple of weeks now, not a wink.

Paul   Why is that? Problems at work?

Charles   Time to call it a night.

Paul   Tell me a joke.

Charles   A joke? How many of those beers you put back?

Paul   In America, all the Blacks are comedians.

Charles   Just because I'm African-American doesn't mean I'm any good at jokes.

Paul (*laughs*)   American, yes. African, no!

Pause. **Charles** *is taken aback.*

Paul   Now, c'mon, a joke!

Charles   I don't know any.

Paul   Lies. C'mon. C'mon, let's hear one!

Charles   Fine. Dan, this reporter friend of mine, told me this one once. There's an old sea captain, he walks into a bar, and the captain, right, right, the captain's completely naked, head to toe, except, except, well he's got on his captain's hat, obviously, so he's not like completely naked. Oh, and he's got, right right, he's got, I think, yes, an anchor and he's gotta an anchor tied to his balls. And the anchor, it's hanging there. The captain walks up to the bartender and says,

(*In a sea captain's voice.*) 'Argh, I'll have me some ale.'

And the bartender politely says, 'Uh sorry, we don't have ale. Beer?'

(*In a sea captain's voice.*) 'Argh, that'll do.'

The bartender gives him the beer, um, and then the captain sits on the stool with his beer. And the whole time, the bartender can't help but notice the anchor, y'know, the anchor tied to his balls. After so, um, time passes the bartender finally gets up the nerve to ask him about it, about the, um, anchor.

'Hey, can't help but notice, but you got an anchor hangin' off yer balls. Why?'

The old sea captain thinks a moment and then replies,

(*In a sea captain's voice.*) 'Argh, it's drivin' me nuts!'

Paul *takes a beat. Then laughs. It does not sound convincing.*

Paul   That is good, Charles.

Charles   Oh wait, wait, shit! It's not an anchor, it's a wheel, it's the ship's wheel that's hanging off his –

Fuck it. I told you I was no good at jokes.

Paul   I have a joke for you. A Tutsi comes home. And he hears noises, noises coming from bedroom. He fears the worst. The house, it is completely black. He lights a match and finds a knife in the kitchen. But all he can find is a small knife. Not a big knife for meat, a small knife –

Charles   A butter knife?

Paul   Yes, yes, butter knife. So this Tutsi goes into the bedroom, with his butter knife. And he sees on the floor, the glint of machete. His heart goes

BOOM BOOM

BOOM BOOM

And he throws open the curtain to let the light in from the street, so he can see who is in there. And there, there in bed with his wife is a big Hutu. The Tutsi, he sighs a sigh of relief:

WHOOSH, I was worried something bad was happening!

The big Hutu looks up at the scared Tutsi holding the little knife, a little knife that cannot even cut a vegetable, and the Hutu tells him, 'Do not fear. Once I am through with your wife, I'll take care of you.'

Dead silence.

Charles   Is that supposed to be funny?

Paul *laughs loudly.*

Paul   You want to survive here you will need a Tutsi's sense of humor.

Charles   Like I said, I'm not into jokes.

Paul   I know the cause of your problem with sleep.

Charles   Do you now?

Paul   The government tells me about your problems.

Charles   Yeah? What did your bosses tell you about me?

Paul   Seems you have been in a bit of trouble.

Pause.

Charles   Can't always believe what you hear.

Paul   What they say is not true, then?

Charles   Let's get this clear. I made a mistake. It was a simple one.

Paul   Stealing other people's words doesn't sound like a simple mistake when words are your business.

Charles   I don't need to defend myself to you.

Paul   My intent is not to anger you.

Charles   Then what is this about?

Paul   Your bosses must be concerned.

Charles   It'll blow over. I'm not worried.

Paul   Your face says otherwise.

Pause.

Paul   Charles, I want to be a friend. I only mention this because, your story about the nuns must be important to you.

Charles   I screwed up, yes. I lost the trust of my editor, my readers. I don't deny it. But this story, about the nuns, this changes all of that.

Paul   Then let me give you some advice. Do not trust these nuns.

Shift.

Charles (*into his recorder*)   Wednesday, March 31st, 1999. The guide the government assigned to me was supposed to take me directly to the jail. He stops at the church where the nuns lived and he shoots a dog. Then takes me on some wild goose chase as punishment for refusing to go inside, making me late.

But I finally met them.

After all those months of paperwork and red tape, after everyone else telling me to let it go, I did it, I'm finally here.

It's wrong what they're doing to these nuns. Making them pay for the crimes of others. I don't know if they're entirely without blame. But my gut's telling me they're scapegoats. How could nuns burn women and children alive? How could they stand idly by and let that shit happen? At least in Belgium, they might get a fair trial.

I'm gonna make you proud with this one. I'll show the world these nuns are innocent. And that I'm still the reporter you taught me to be.

Shift. A home in Kigali.

Dusabi   Is he here?

Paul   I took him to the church. But he will not go inside.

Dusabi   Can you blame the reporter for not wanting to see?

Pause.

Paul   I was hoping you would meet us at the bar as we discussed.

Dusabi   Did you tell him about me?

Paul   You asked me not to. Even my superiors do not know. I keep your promise, but Dusabi, you must see that your story, told in the right way, it could –

Dusabi   My story? I will not speak to a stranger about my life.

Paul   Think of what it could mean.

Dusabi   Look at me, Paul. It takes everything from me. Who I should speak to is the nuns.

Paul   The nuns were supposed to go. Not turn into this story. He stirs up trouble, this journalist. Rwandans should judge Rwandans. The nuns should be tried here.

Dusabi   The government is concerned?

Paul   The story of the nuns could change opinions. The Americans do not want to read about the crimes of nuns. They want to imagine they are somehow free of sin. I can see, in his eyes, he will show kindness to them.

Dusabi   Then why allow him to speak to them?

Paul   This paper, *The New York Times*, attacks our government in print. They call our prisons unfair.

Dusabi   I should be able to look the nuns in the eye and speak to them –

Paul   I understand your reasons why you do not wish the government to know. You would have to testify in Belgium, this is true. But speak to Charles, tell him what you know. Your story confirms the RPF claims. There is no need for you to testify.

Dusabi   I want to speak to the nuns.

Paul   Dusabi, my hands are tied. No one can see the nuns except for Charles. My superiors would put someone else in charge of him if I disobeyed.

Dusabi   This reporter, he cannot, cannot think them innocent.

Paul   Talk to him.

Dusabi   My mind is made up.

Paul   Do you not want justice?

Dusabi   Justice will not bring back my wife.

Blackout.

Day Two

A holding cell in the jail.

Sister Justina   I do not have long. The guard will be back soon.

Sister Alice   I slept. The doctor gave me a pill.

Sister Justina   And you feel better?

Sister Alice   Yes. Thank you.

Sister Justina   What happened, Consolata?

Sister Alice   I just felt faint, that is all.

Sister Justina   You do not take care of yourself. Do not sleep. Get yourself so upset.

Remember the violence of men is something to push away from sight.

Sister Alice   I grow so anxious. And you were angry at me for talking about Father's vision.

Sister Justina   The less we speak about Father the better.

Sister Alice   But what are we to speak of?

Sister Justina   You must think with the stranger's ears. Consider what he will think. Imagine you tell him the Virgin Mother's words to Father, imagine how he will hear it in a way different than it was intended.

Sister Alice   I don't know what to do. Look, my hand still shakes.

Sister Justina   You do not have to speak to him today.

Pause.

Sister Alice   Did he see me faint?

Sister Justina   The reporter? You collapsed in front of him. He called the guards. He was concerned for you. I could see.

Sister Alice   He is a handsome man, this Charles.

Sister Justina   He has the face of a boy. Let me speak for us.

Sister Alice   He might feel sympathy for me, if I speak to him today.

Sister Justina   We are not deceivers, Consolata.

Sister Alice   You said he showed concern. He must be on our side. He is our only hope, Bernadette. Tutsis want blood. Doesn't matter here, doesn't matter Belgium. They will punish us. They will do anything to see / us suffer anything –

Sister Justina   Do not get upset.

Sister Alice   What should we tell him? What story?

Sister Justina   It is not a story. It is the truth.

Sister Alice   Then tell me what to do.

Sister Justina   You should speak honestly to him. But you do not have to answer certain questions. More difficult subjects. I will speak on those.

Sister Alice   What if, what if we tell events in a way that shows us / in the best possible –?

Sister Justina   Consolata. Consolata. The truth is what will set us free.

Sister Alice   We will live out our remaining days in places such as this, won't we?

Sister Justina   This place cannot make us hard. We are the same as when we came here. God will provide a way out of this. You must trust in Him. You must trust in me.

Shift. An interrogation room in the jail.

Sister Justina   Shall we begin?

Charles *switches on the Dictaphone.*

Charles   April 1st. Holy Thursday.

Sister Justina   You remember.

Charles   April Fools' Day too. At least back in the States.

Sister Justina   There are no fools sitting here.

Charles   Have you ever left Rwanda before?

Sister Justina   No, never.

Charles   It's hard being a stranger in a strange place.

Sister Justina   This jail is my teacher.

Charles   Yes.

The two share a look.

Charles   The day before President Habyarimana's death. Was there anything unusual?

Sister Justina   The day before the President's death, men came to visit Father.

Charles   Was this unusual?

Sister Justina   There were many. Their coming, felt, important.

Charles   What did these men want?

Sister Justina   I do not know. They request a meeting with Father Neromba.

Charles   Did this concern you?

Sister Justina   I want to make this clear. Sister Alice and I, we are not Father Neromba. His actions are not our actions.

Charles   Understood.

Sister Justina   Father is no longer here and we are always asked to explain his actions.

Charles   What happened after the men visit the parish?

Sister Justina   The next day, the miracle. There is much celebrating at the parish that day. Then Seth comes at night

and tells us the news, the President's death. It is upsetting.
Our President, dead. Such a loss. And I worry what might
happen because of it.

Charles   Why, Sister?

Sister Justina   I remember earlier troubles between Hutus
and Tutsis. Next morning, I hear gunfire. I go to the kitchen
and the food deliveries do not come. And then . . .

They begin to arrive. People from nearby towns, from
Kigali, the Don Bosco school.

Charles   The UN were stationed there, at Don Bosco,
before they withdrew.

Sister Justina   We do not know such things. There was no
radio, no outside communication.

Charles   And these people, they were all Tutsis?

Sister Justina   Yes, they were Tutsis. At first, it is only a few.
By evening, hundreds.

Charles   Why do they come to your church?

Sister Justina   The church is a safe place.

Charles   Did you speak to them? They tell you what was
happening?

Sister Justina   There wasn't time.
Charles, a few were cut
Bleeding
I do not know what has happened to them.

Charles   Sister, imagine you're in my shoes for a moment.
And you hear that. Hundreds of people arriving at your
church, some wounded. My first thought is –

Sister Justina   I cannot concern myself with how this
happens. My first thought is to take care of them. But. We
were not equipped to take care of injuries like those. We
make rice. We feed them. Then the men from Kigali arrive.

Charles   The *interahamwe*? The Hutu militias?

Sister Justina   These men, they are not strangers to me.

Charles   And these are the same men that visited Father two days before?

Sister Justina   I told you I was not involved in any meeting.

Charles   But when the men return, what is it they want?

Sister Justina   They tell us: Go only to the kitchen. Do not go inside the church.
We obey.

Charles   Did they threaten you?

Sister Justina   No, Charles. These men know me. They call me Sister. I know them since they were boys, only this high off the earth.

Charles   But these men are part of the *interahamwe*.

Sister Justina   There was war. Between us and the RPF. And my job, Charles, is take care of the spiritual needs of the parish.

Charles   The court charges that you aided the *interahamwe* in murdering hundreds of Tutsis who took shelter at your church.

Sister Justina   We kill no Tutsis.

Charles   *Inyenzi*. Cockroach. Is that what these men called the Tutsis?

Sister Justina   Good men can be misled.

Charles   The RPF government contests your statements.

Sister Justina   No.

Charles   They claim you were aware of the plans. That you aided the militia.

Sister Justina   Not true.

Charles   Did you give the men fuel?

Sister Justina   You are not understanding me.

Charles   Sister Justina, did these men threaten you?

Sister Justina *looks away.*

Charles   Help me out here, Sister. Think about Sister Alice.

Sister Justina *locks eyes with* **Charles**.

Sister Justina   We did not know what was to happen to those people in the church. We are taken away into the hills before the killings begin. We know nothing. That is the truth.

Shift. Later in the interrogation room.

Charles   How are you feeling, Sister?

Sister Alice   Much better. Thank you.

Charles   You mentioned yesterday the miracle.

Sister Alice   It is silly.

Charles   It was a special day. Father Neromba must've been touched, to have such a visit.

Sister Alice   Yes.

Charles   Tell me about it.

Pause.

Sister Alice   Father took his morning walks and on that day when he returned, tears flowed from his eyes, he took my hand, saying: She came to me. The Virgin Mother. She came to me.

Charles   What did the Virgin Mother say?

Sister Alice   I do not, remember.

Charles (*referring to Dictaphone*)   I'm going to shut this off. Look.

Charles *shuts off the recorder.*

Sister Alice Why do you want to know about this?

Charles The Virgin Mary came to Father. It's a miracle. How could I not want to know?

Sister Alice You *are* a Catholic, aren't you, Charles?

Charles Tell me about Father.

Sister Alice He took good care of Sister and I.

Charles When did you last see him?

Sister Alice Not since the day we were sent into the hills. He stayed behind at the church.

Charles Did Father ever use the word *inyenzi* to describe the Tutsis?

Silence.

Sister Alice He is a good man.

Charles Does a good man allow the massacre of hundreds of innocent Tutsis at his church?

Sister Alice We were not there.

Charles Yesterday, when you fainted, I saw, in your eyes such pain.

Sister Alice I was weak with hunger, that is all. They barely keep us alive here.

Charles There's no one here. Recorder's off. Just you and me, talking.

Silence.

Charles Sister Alice, do you understand the seriousness of the charges against you?

They claim you helped the militia. That you murdered Tutsis. Do you know what will happen to you if they find you guilty? Do you?

Sister Alice   Yes.

Charles   Then I suggest you talk.

Pause.

Sister Alice   Father did use that word. *Inyenzi.* But his own mother was Tutsi. He cannot hate the Tutsis the way you think. People say things. For protection.

Charles   Did he call his mother an *inyenzi*?

Sister Alice   It is only a word.

Charles   And what did the Virgin Mary say to Father?

Sister Alice   She told Father. She told him, she told him the day of judgment was at hand. Those who repent will be saved. And those who don't. They will be, cast out.

Charles   This happened the day after the militias came to visit Father?

Sister Alice   Charles, the Tutsis arrive at the church and we take care of them as best we can then the next day, we are taken to the hills and never return to our home.

Charles   While you were at the church, no murders took place?

Sister Alice   The injured arrive. We take care of them. The men come and we are sent away.

Charles   You are not answering the question.

Sister Alice   I do not understand –

Charles   I think you do.

Pause.

Charles   Sister Alice, you could spend the next four decades of your life in jail, maybe more, if you don't talk to me.

Sister Alice   The night before we leave . . .

Sister Alice *trails off. Silence.*

Sister Alice   The night before we leave, the sound of the
crying, it never ceases, Charles. I try to sleep in the rectory,
I cannot.
. . .
There was a boy. Vincent. Eight or nine. Face like an angel.
His mother and father, he watched them be murdered. He
comes to the church with neighbors that day. He comes to
me. Calls me, Mother.
I say, Vincent, I am not your mother.
He says, Yes, you are.
Vincent, I am not your –
Yes, you are.
That day, he helps me in the kitchen, with the washing up.
He would take my hand.
I say, I have to work, Vincent, you must let go of my hand,
you must return to the church.
He have none of it. He follows me, puts his small fingers
in mine.
He says, Mother, you must hold my hand, if you let go,
something bad will happen. I know you. You will not let go.
I have no children. That is the price of this life.
We are told we will be leaving the next morning before the
sun rises.
I think about Vincent.
That night, it begins. The men, they come into the church.
They take a few of the old ones. I hear these sounds out in
the hills
Horrible horrible sounds
Father said they wouldn't hurt the children –
Vincent
I go downstairs, to the church. Cannot find Vincent.
I run into the hills. Two men hold him down.
No, Not Him, He's My Son
I say those words
Not Him He's Mine Not. My. Son.

Grab me, thinking they've got another one, one they missed.
Father stops them.
Says, That Tutsi shit's not hers,
What you saying Consolata?
This is Sister Alice, Sister Alice
Vincent's crying, Mommy don't let them kill me I'll never be
Tutsi again,
Mommy Mommy Mommy
No, no, please don't,
They bring it down on his scalp
One
Two
Splashes all over the earth
Bursting on the ground
His smile
His teeth
His precious head
His light
His.
. . .
. . .
I never cry. Won't now.
I walk down that hill, I go to the kitchen, I wash dishes, I
make rice
Can't eat, smell's too much.
That morning, we leave the church.
I carry this inside and now tell only you.

Sister Alice *begins to cry.*

Charles *touches her gently.*

Sister Alice   I knew what was coming.

Shift. A hotel bar in Kigali.

Paul   My friend will be here soon. You'll see.

Charles   What's this about, Paul?

Paul   You'll see.

Charles   Hold up, listen, I got a fax from the news desk back in New York. There's some chatter about Hutu priests being sheltered at Catholic churches in Texas. It might be worth telling your people. I know you're trying to track down Father Neromba.

Paul   That is helpful information.

Charles   Pass it along to superiors.

Paul   He will be found.

Charles   I hope so.

Pause.

Paul   Why do you do this? This kind of work. Why?

Charles   Why am I a journalist?

Paul   My work. It makes sense. But yours?

Charles   It's a job. Plain and simple.

Paul   I do not believe that.

Charles   My job's to listen. That's what I prefer to do. Listen.

Paul   Just curious that's all. Your father do this job too?

Charles   No, no. Nothing like that.

Paul   My father was a farmer. I try and remember him. They say he was a good man. I must take their word. Some days it is hard to know that I will never see him again.

Pause.

Charles   As a kid, I had this obsession with *Life* magazine. You know it?

Paul *nods his head 'no'.*

Charles   It chronicles the world, in pictures. When I was in high school, I found this old issue, in some box in our

basement. There was a photograph in it. A photograph of a
lynching in Mississippi.
This crowd of onlookers
one looking right at the camera
a man in a tie
finger pointing to two Black men hanging from a tree
blood on their necks
dripping down like chocolate syrup.
Ain't no red in a black and white photograph.
My dad grew up in the South. Couldn't even look at that
picture.
But I'd stare at it, thinking: this is what people do to each
other.
This is what people do.

Paul   You grow in a dark place, my friend.

Charles   I go where horrible shit happens, talk to people,
write it down and tell the readers what they don't want to
hear. That's what Dan taught me.

Paul   Dan?

Charles   When I joined the paper, he taught me
everything. Taught me what we do matters

Dan made me a better reporter. And I gotta get that back.

Paul   What does your wife back home think of your job?

Charles   OK, OK, enough questions, man.

Paul   Ah, I get you! You have many girlfriends. Do not like
to have just one.

Charles   No, nothing like that.
I was with someone. Kendra. But –

Paul   She leave you, huh?

Charles   Not exactly. It's a complicated situation.

Paul   What is complicated about a woman?

Charles   You obviously don't know American women.

Paul   Your Kendra is complicated?

Charles   We work together, she and I. She's my editor. It was a stupid thing to do. You spend nights at the office together. Things happen.

Paul   Do you love her?

Charles   See you tomorrow.

Paul   Where are you going?

Charles   Time to pack it in.

Paul   Nonono, wait, another beer!

Charles   Not a chance. Five's my limit.

Dusabi *enters the bar.* **Paul** *sees him.*

Paul   Dusabi, you come.

Dusabi   Paul.

Paul   This is Charles.

Charles   Hello.

Dusabi   Yes.

Paul   Charles, this is Dusabi.

Dusabi   Paul.

Paul   I am glad you come. Please, Dusabi. Sit. Join us.

Charles   Everything OK?

Paul   Charles I make you an offer –

Dusabi *attacks* **Charles** *with surprising violence.*

Dusabi   Where Were You When We Were Dying By The Thousands?

Paul   Dusabi, stop –

Paul *stops* **Dusabi**.

Charles   Listen, I don't know what Paul's / been telling you –

Dusabi   You come here now. Why?

Charles   Because I'm a journalist and there's a / story here.

Paul   Charles, listen, Dusabi was at the church.

Charles   I don't understand.

Paul   Dusabi and his wife Elisabeth took shelter at the church where the nuns lived. They were left for dead.

Dusabi   Paul, please.

Charles   I was told there were no survivors from the massacre.

Dusabi   You were told incorrect.

Paul   That's what people believe. But he and Elisabeth survived. Dusabi, he prefers not to speak at the trial.

Charles   You survived?

Dusabi   I live, yes.

Paul   Dusabi is your story.

Charles   Is this some kind of trick?

Paul   No trick. We must talk.

The lights in the bar flicker and go black.

Charles   What's happening?

Paul   Power failure.

Paul *flicks on his lighter.*

Paul   This will help.

Charles   Are you telling me the truth? Did you survice the massacre at the church?

Paul   Charles, we must speak directly. I know that your career is not what it was because of the scandal. You were the young star and now all that is changing thanks to this problem.

Charles   It's gonna blow over.

Paul   Are you sure of that?

Pause.

The lights flicker back on.

Paul   We know this story is very important to you.

Charles   I believe in this story.

Paul   But what is the story your bosses want you to tell?

Charles   I worked hard to get here.

Paul   Then you do not want to ruin this opportunity. Because the nuns are not your story. Dusabi is. And Dusabi will speak to you because I make it possible. But the nuns cannot look innocent. They are guilty, Charles.

Dusabi   I make a mistake coming here tonight.

Paul   Dusabi, wait. You need to tell the world. This must never happen again.

Dusabi   You have more faith in men than I do.

Paul   Now, what does Charles have? Only the word of the nuns.

Father Neromba, missing. The Hutu militias, who believes a word they say? But what you say, Dusabi, that will change minds.

Charles, perhaps, an arrangement can be made. Names, changed, if need be.

Charles   All I want is the truth.

Dusabi   You have come to the wrong place, my friend, if you are looking for truth.

Shift.

Charles (*into the recorder*)   Almost morning. Can't get my thoughts to shut off. There's a bigger story here than I even suspected. The older nun, I don't know, but she's not telling me everything. And Sister Alice, she told me she saw the killing start, tried to save a boy. If you were here, you might warn me, tell me my eyes are getting clouded by wanting to prove their innocence. I know that's the story Kendra wants. And that younger nun, looks just like her. And that makes me wanna believe Christ. I know I can't trust this guide Paul and yet . . . if this man at the bar tonight is . . . Christ. Should at least try and sleep.

Shift. A home in Kigali.

Paul   You should not have struck him.

Dusabi   When I saw him, the rage –

Paul   We need this story to come out correct.

Dusabi   That is your concern, not mine.

Paul   I will bring him here to your home tomorrow, and you will speak to him.

Dusabi   Time and time again, I close my eyes and see what happened those awful days. Each time, it feels new, happening all over again. I cannot talk to a stranger about this.

Paul   Much is at stake here, Dusabi. The younger nun, she is / telling him –

Dusabi   I don't think I can, Paul.

Paul   The younger nun told him she tried to save a child at the church.

Dusabi   How do you know this? He tells you this?

Paul   His interviews are being recorded. My job is to listen to the tapes / and report what is said –

Dusabi   Do not tell me this. I do not want to know.

Paul   You must listen. They find the nuns not guilty, there is a chance, actual chance, that all prisoners will go free. This thing has been discussed. Amnesty, they call it.
Reconciliation. That will not happen. The murderers of my family, your friends, Elisabeth –

Dusabi   This cannot happen.

Paul   I told my supervising officers about you today. I told them I knew of a survivor. I am to tell you that you must speak with the reporter.

Dusabi   Your promise, Paul, you promised me –

Paul   I will not let these nuns go free.

Dusabi   But what you ask, I cannot –

Paul   They are not asking, Dusabi.

Dusabi *registers what* **Paul** *is saying.*

Paul   I protected you as much as I can. You will not go to Belgium. But you must do this. Or there'll be consequences for both of us.

Blackout.

Day Three

An interrogation room in the jail.

Sister Alice   How can I trust you?

Charles   I come here only to learn the truth.

Sister Alice   The things I tell you, you mustn't tell Sister Justina. Bernadette is set in her ways. She obeys. I obey the teachings of God, but I know the ways of the Church, they are not always the ways of God. And if she learned what I was sharing with you, she would be very cross with me. She thinks I can be, foolish.

And here, in this jail, I could be at risk, of some violence, if it was known what I will tell you.

Charles   You have my word. What you tell me remains between us.

Sister Alice   The night Vincent was killed. The men, when they go away, when it is late, when it is quiet, I go to the church. I find some supplies in the closet. Flashlight, canteen. No one sees me. I am so scared. My hands, they shake. Like they do now. Shake just at the thought. I go to the church. And take a few of the Tutsis aside. I give them the supplies, tell them about a barn up in the hills, where they can go and hide. I can only help a few.

Charles   Sister, you helped Tutsis escape? Do you know what this means if that appears in print before your trial?

Sister Alice   I could not save Vincent, at least I can help his neighbors, his friends.

Charles   What happened to them?

Sister Alice   I do not know.

Charles   Did Sister Justina help you?

Sister Alice   She does not know what I've done. I cannot tell her. Imagine. Disobeying Father. Risking my life for Tutsis.

Charles   What are Sister Justina's views of the Tutsis?

Sister Alice   She is older.

But this, you must ask her.

Charles   You have told no one this?

Sister Alice   How many *interahamwe* live in this jail with me? You know what they did to Hutu traitors. And yet you ask me that?

Charles   Your lawyers?

Sister Alice   That a woman, a girl, could do this? The Tutsis in power do not want to hear about the Hutu nun who helps a few Tutsis. They want to see us all shamed.

Charles   I need evidence.

Sister Alice   Charles, you are smart, do not be stupid. I do not ask names. I do not know what happen to them. I wish one of them would come forward and speak of what I did for them. But perhaps they are not still in this world to speak for me. No one remains from the church except Sister and I.

Pause.

Sister Alice   I see in your eyes, Charles. You want to believe.

Shift. A home in Kigali.

Dusabi   I make no promises.

Charles   I understand your hesitation –

Dusabi   I have questions.

Charles   Will your wife be joining us?

Dusabi   Elisabeth is dead.

Pause.

Charles   I'm sorry, Dusabi. Paul didn't –

Dusabi   In the years after, she could not go on. She was
never herself. They cut her at the arms. But she lived. How?
I do not know. She was a big woman, my Elisabeth, strong.
But last year, her light went out. She passed in her sleep.

Charles   If you're the only one left who can tell what
happened at that church, then you have an obligation,
Dusabi.

Dusabi   Yes, Paul likes to tell me about my, obligations.

Charles   It can take away some of the pain, telling me
what happened.

Dusabi   You go to lots of places like Rwanda?

Charles   Somalia, Bosnia, the West Bank, it's what I do.

Dusabi   Dangerous.

Charles   Sometimes.

Dusabi   Is this merely another story for you? Another
interview?

Charles   No. It's not. I fought to come here because this
story is important to me.

Dusabi   For your career? Paul tells me of your troubles.

Charles   That's not what this is about.

Dusabi   Then tell me what this is about. To tell what I
know, I need to know the man I am telling.

Pause.

Dusabi   I see how it is. You want me to talk, but you will not
talk to me. You should go.

Charles   Dan. That's why this story matters so much to me.
But I don't see why / that matters to you –

Dusabi   Tell me. Please.

Charles   Dan was a reporter. No, more than that. He was a friend. A mentor. We were both working Mogadishu back in '93.

A mob of Somalis. Smashed Dan's face in with rocks. Wrong place, wrong time. I was always with him, but that day I wasn't.

Dusabi   Lucky.

Charles   Funny. Don't feel lucky. His death hit me hard. But I pushed ahead, thought I was OK. But last few months, I've been thinking about him a lot.

And work. It's been hard. I've made mistakes.

Dusabi   Did you come here to tell the world the nuns are innocent?

Charles   An article with some hope, that's not a terrible thing to want.

I think there's a chance they're innocent of these charges. Especially the younger one.

Dusabi   I do not think the innocent have so much blood on their hands.

Charles   If you are telling me the truth, then you are the only person left to tell what happened inside that church.

Dusabi   Most days, I can't eat a thing. Vomit it all back up. A smell in my nostrils I will never shake.
I was dead, Charles.
But I return. Resurrected. For what?

Charles   To tell your truth.

Dusabi   If I tell you, you must do something for me.

Charles   Of course.

Dusabi   Come back tonight.

Charles   How do I know I can trust you?

Dusabi   You think I would lie?

Charles   Paul, the RPF, there must be pressure. And I can't go back with a story filled with half-truths if I'm going to survive at the paper. If it turned out my story isn't accurate, I'm finished.

I need proof.

Dusabi *stands and begins to remove his shirt.*

Dusabi   The proof you ask for . . .

Charles   Wait, Dusabi . . . please, I didn't mean . . . you don't / have to –

Dusabi   You ask if I speak the truth, then look.

There are thick scars on both of **Dusabi**'s *arms and a scar that cuts across his abdomen.*

Charles *looks.*

Dusabi   My body is proof of what I say.

Shift. An interrogation room in the jail.

Charles   What was happening in the church the night before you left?

Sister Justina   I do what I am told. I stay away. Then we are taken into the hills.

Charles   What are your thoughts about the Tutsis?

Sister Justina   We are both part of God's plan.

Charles   The Tutsis in your church were injured. Couldn't leave, they were trapped. And you knew the men could return to do more harm.

Sister Justina   I was scared, Charles. I wish I could say I was brave. You see it, you turn away, because you do not have power. I am a woman. It might be hard as a man to understand. Have you ever felt that? Like you had no power? Helpless?

Charles   I have, yes.

Sister Justina   Then you know what a terrible terrible feeling that is.

And are you guilty of a crime because of it?

Charles   Sometimes, I feel I might be.

Sister Justina   That is not what God would want.

Charles   Once I was frightened and didn't stay to make sure a friend got out of a situation safely, and he did, Sister. And maybe if I hadn't run . . .

Sister Justina   You were frightened?

Charles   Sister, I was terrified.

Sister Justina   Then we are the same, Charles.

Charles   Did you give them fuel? The *interahamwe*?

Sister Justina   They did ask for supplies, yes.

Charles   They had weapons. They threatened you.

Sister Justina   No, Charles.

Charles   This is not a story that will change the hearts of my readers.

Sister Justina   My story may not be one of courage. But I always obeyed. That is our way.

Charles   What did you give them?

Sister Justina   Supplies. I don't remember what.

Charles   Fuel?

Sister Justina   What does it matter?

Charles   They burned people alive, Sister. I might've run, left my friend behind. But I didn't give the mob the rocks to smash his face to pulp.

Shift. A cell in the jail.

Sister Justina (*singing softly to herself*)
> *Jesus loves me*
> *This I know*
> *Because the Bible tells me so*
> *Little ones to Him belong*
> *For they are weak*
> *But He is strong . . .*

Paul *has entered quietly. She senses his presence and turns to see him.*

Paul   Do not let me stop you.

Sister Justina   Good Friday today. Should be at the church, preparing for services, but instead I am here in this filthy place.

Paul   Your church is a graveyard. There are no services there.

Silence.

Sister Justina   Where is the guard?

Paul   I come with news.

Sister Justina   I know who you are, soldier.

Paul   You will be leaving for Belgium by weekend's end.

Sister Justina   No.

Paul   We received word today from the Belgian authorities.

Sister Justina   I do not understand, we are told our trial is not for weeks.

Paul   There's much, Sister, in this world I do not understand.

Sister Justina   You look at me with such hatred.

Paul   I see who you are.

Sister Justina   I am sorry you feel such a way.

Paul   And when you see me, you see a cockroach, someone's life not worth saving? That song, is that what you sang as my people were murdered in your church?

Sister Justina   I bear no ill will to any Tutsi.

Paul   How do you answer to God for what you did?

Sister Justina   I know God's love.

Paul   My God has no love for you.

Sister Justina   I'll pray tonight God forgives you for saying such a thing.

Paul   This story. Talking to this reporter. It will not help you. You think he is on your side?

Sister Justina   Charles is a good man.

Paul   You Hutus are the vermin should be wiped from the earth.

Sister Justina   You should leave.

Paul *takes out a sharpened knife.*

Paul   A gift, Sister.

Sister Justina   I have no need of such a thing.

Paul   There is still time to do the honorable thing.

Sister Justina   Look at me when you say that. Do not place it there and walk away. Look at me.

You do not even know me. You do not even ask my name. Do not even give me the chance to defend myself. You think you know. No need to ask questions.

But I can tell you soldier, I know your name. I hear the reporter call you Paul. And Paul, I do not hate you, even when you come here with this gift. Because I know you speak from a place of hurt. And when you go home, if not tonight, some night in the future, you will know that, in anger, you punished innocents like me unjustly for the crimes of others. And that, that will be on your conscience until you take your last breath.

Paul *finally looks at* **Sister Justina**.

Paul   Save the speeches for the Belgians, Bernadette.

Shift.

Charles (*into the recorder*)   Friday evening. I feel the burden the longer I'm here. If there's even a hint of doubt in my article about their innocence, what future might I be condemning them to? I try not to see the nuns who taught me at school when I speak to them, I try not to see Kendra. But how can I not want to see goodness?

I know truth is always the goal. But we can't always achieve it. And sometimes we choose not to report the truth, because we see the impact it could have.

Given the hot water I'm now in, that's a dangerous thing to admit, I know, but c'mon, you and I both know it happens.

This survivor. Accounts say no one survived the massacre at that church. But what if? Even if he wasn't there, the scars on his body, the look in his eyes.

I speak to him tonight.

Shift. A home in Kigali.

Dusabi   I will be walking, thinking my head is clear, and then turn a corner and then I am there again, in that place.

Charles   Ever since I got here, all this stuff keeps flooding my head. Things I thought I'd dealt with. But listen. My life, my problems, it's nothing.

Dusabi   We act as if there is a way to measure grief. But this is a thing for which no measure exists.

Charles   I screwed up. I stole another journalist's words. Who'll ever believe me now?

Dusabi   And you've come here to make amends?

Charles   That wasn't the intention. I thought it would be a great story, a good exclusive for the paper. But now, wrongs need to be righted, and not just mine.

Pause. **Dusabi** *observes* **Charles**.

Dusabi   I will tell you what happened to Elisabeth and I.

Charles *goes to start his Dictaphone.*

Charles   May I record this –?

Dusabi   No, Charles, to know what I know you must do more than listen.

Close your eyes.

Charles *does.*

Dusabi   I want you to see what I tell you. You understand?

I want you to picture our journey to the school Don Bosco. Elisabeth and I. Our journey that ends at the church.

Charles   You first went to Don Bosco, where the UN was stationed?

Dusabi   The Blue Helmets, yes.

We were home. There was tension in the air. I know not how to describe it.

Sound: the distant crackle of a radio.

Dusabi   The announcement comes on the radio, I feel frightened. President Habyarimana's plane has been shot down. All those onboard have perished. I hear the news and I cry out, Elisabeth!

Charles   Elisabeth.

Dusabi   That's right. I cry out for Elisabeth.
Elisabeth. I tell her, We must go, we must leave here.
I look out the window. I see the roadblocks going up.

Sound: the distant sound of trucks.

Dusabi   Men enter into the houses of our neighbors. I tell Elisabeth we must go to the Blue Helmets. To Don Bosco. There is no time to even gather our things. On the radio, they call out names. Names of people who they say are traitors. I know these names. They are not traitors. These are neighbors, friends.

Sound: a radio DJ calling out names (in Kinyarwandan) of Tutsis and Hutu sympathizers, telling his listeners, 'Muhere aruhande.'

Dusabi   The DJ tells his listeners

(*Speaking with the voice from the radio.*) 'Go about the task,

Go about the task from one place to another until the work is done.'

Then

The radio goes suddenly silent.

Dusabi   The power is cut.

The lights flicker and go dim. **Dusabi** *and* **Charles** *are faintly visible in the darkness.*

Dusabi   We decide to exit in the cover of dark and hurry to the school. I tell Elisabeth we will be safe at the school with the protection of the Blue Helmets

Yes, safe at Don Bosco

On the journey we see horrible sights

I cry out: *Mana wari uri he?*

Charles   God, why have you forsaken me?

Dusabi   Yes

And I think to myself

The weight of what is to come is unbearable

It is crushing me

But Elisabeth and I continue. And at dawn, we arrive at the school.

Lights return.

Shift. The Don Bosco School.

Charles *sits, eyes closed.*

In the school, **Dusabi** *stands with* **Sister Justina** *and* **Paul**. **Sister Justina** *speaks for Elisabeth.* **Paul** *speaks for Pierre.* (**Paul** *speaks with a French accent.*)

Paul (*as Pierre*)   You are at Don Bosco, friends. You are safe here. UN Forces control the building. The militia cannot enter.

Dusabi   Will you help us?

Paul (*as Pierre*)   Our mission is to protect you. The United Nations will not fail you.

Dusabi   Friend, what is your name?

Paul (*as Pierre*)   Corporal Dupont. Call me Pierre.

Dusabi   Pierre, I am Dusabi.

Sister Justina (*as Elisabeth*)   I am Elisabeth. You must help us. They control the streets

Dusabi   Killing anyone they think is Tutsi –

Sister Justina (*as Elisabeth*)   I saw children, old women, throats slit, skulls smashed, lying by the road

Dusabi   They call out our names on the radio

Sister Justina (*as Elisabeth*)   Shout them on the street

Dusabi   The Hutus want to wipe us off the earth

Sister Justina (*as Elisabeth*)   It is the end of the world.

Paul (*as Pierre*)   I swear to you

On my life

Nothing bad will happen to you here.

Sound: loud gunfire and screams in the distance.

Shift.

Dusabi   What is happening?

Paul (*as Pierre*)   There has been an incident.

Dusabi   Tell me.

Paul (*as Pierre*)   Ten of our soldiers . . .

Dusabi   What is it, Pierre?

Paul (*as Pierre*)   They were told not to fire. That is not our mission. But the militias –

Dusabi   Cut –

Sister Justina (*as Elisabeth*)   I am sorry

Dusabi   Slashed –

Sister Justina (*as Elisabeth*)   So sorry –

Dusabi   Burnt –

Paul (*as Pierre*)   We are withdrawing.

Dusabi   No, you cannot.

Sister Justina (*as Elisabeth*)   I do not understand.

Paul (*as Pierre*)   The UN is withdrawing all of its peacekeeping troops.

Dusabi   Do you know what will happen to us if you go?

Paul (*as Pierre*)   All Western aid workers, all American and European citizens, all troops are leaving, effective immediately.

Sister Justina (*as Elisabeth*)   No! You Cannot! You Cannot Go!

Paul (*as Pierre*)   There is nothing I can do –

Dusabi   Pierre, please, listen: You have to help us, You must, you must help us, If you leave we will be

Stomped out like cockroaches

Our bodies ground into the earth

Sister Justina (*as Elisabeth*)   You swore to us you would keep us safe, you swore on your life.

Paul (*as Pierre*)   I am sorry.

The corporal leaves.

Dusabi   Corporal!

Silence.

Dusabi   Elisabeth, we have been abandoned.

Sound: loud gunfire, close.

Dusabi   We must go. Flee Kigali. The church on the hill. We must take refuge there. It is not a far walk. If we leave now, we can walk there in cover of dark.

Sister Justina (*as Elisabeth*)   They know the soldiers have left. They are waiting for us. Just outside the gates. Listen. Do you hear them? They will cut us down as we leave.

Dusabi   We will go through the hills, avoid the roads.

Sister Justina (*as Elisabeth*)   Yes.

Dusabi   We will survive this, I promise you.

Dusabi *sees a figure.*

Dusabi   Pierre, you return to help us.

It is **Paul**. *But he speaks for Seth, a member of the* interahamwe.

Paul (*as Seth*) (*Laughs.*)   What you call me, Tutsi?

Dusabi   Elisabeth, come –

Paul (*as Seth*)   You know who I am?

Dusabi   We are leaving.

Please.

Get out of our way.

The interahamwe *spits in* **Dusabi**'s *face.* **Dusabi** *tries to push him out of the way and the* interahamwe *knocks him to the ground.*

Dusabi   You can have our cows. All of them.

I am not a poor man.

Paul (*as Seth*)   Your cattle are already mine.

Dusabi   Our home, our money –

Paul (*as Seth*)   What is your name, cockroach?

Sister Justina (*as Elisabeth*)   Do not hurt him!

Dusabi   Be quiet, Elisabeth.

Paul (*as Seth*)   Name?

Silence.

Dusabi *slowly stands and takes Elisabeth by the hand. They try to exit.*

The interahamwe *blocks them.*

Paul (*as Seth*)   Where do you think you are going?

Sister Justina (*as Elisabeth*)   The church outside / the city –

Dusabi   Elisabeth! Be quiet.

Paul (*as Seth*)   Remember me.

Remember my face.

I am Seth.

And your time is coming.

The interahamwe *takes out a pistol.* **Dusabi** *pushes Elisabeth away.*

Dusabi   Please, spare my wife.

The interahamwe *shoots the pistol into the air.* **Dusabi** *falls in fear.*

Paul (*as Seth, laughs*)   Go to the church, *inyenzi.*

The interahamwe *leaves.*

Dusabi   *Mana / wari uri he?*

Charles   God, Why Have You Forsaken Me?

Shift. A home in Kigali.

Dusabi   I was never so scared as I was that night. We flee in the dark, into the hills, to the church.

Charles   And when you arrive?

Dusabi   There are already hundreds of us there, all taking shelter.

Shift. The church.

Sound: hundreds of men, women and children, crying and terrified.

Dusabi   Elisabeth, we will be safe here in the church.

Sister Justina (*as Elisabeth*)   Yes.

Shift. A home in Kigali and the yard in front of the church.

We hear **Sister Alice** *singing.*

Sister Alice (*singing*)
Jesus loves me
This I know
Because the Bible / tells me so
Little ones to Him belong
For they are weak
But He Is Strong
Yes, Jesus Loves Me
Yes, Jesus Loves Me
Yes, Jesus Loves Me
The Bible tells me so –

Dusabi (*to* **Charles**)   I remember as I try to sleep, I think I hear singing . . .

Pause.

Charles *opens his eyes.*

Charles   What is it, Dusabi?

Paul *appears. He is Seth. He carries a machete and a canister of fuel.*

Charles   The *interahamwe* are coming.

Sister Justina (*as Elisabeth*)   Dusabi.

Dusabi   Elisabeth.

Paul (*as Seth*)   *Inyenzi.*

Charles   No!

Sister Alice *stops singing and covers her ears.*

The deafening sound of the apocalypse. The singing – all sound – no sound – drowned out by this deafening deafening sound . . .

Charles *feels the* interahamwe
slashing his chest with the machete
cutting his tendon
dousing his body in fuel.

He howls and howls.

Charles *sees the* interahamwe
cutting Elisabeth's arms
slicing
slicing
slicing
them to the bone.

Charles *howls and howls.*

The sound cuts out.

Shift. A home in Kigali.

Dusabi *holds* **Charles**.

Charles (*screaming, sobbing*)

Dusabi   . . . it's OK it's OK / it's OK . . .

Charles   . . . I can't I / can't . . .

Dusabi   . . . you're safe / now you're safe . . .

Charles   . . .

Look away, do not see me like this.

Dusabi   I was so close to death, Elisabeth and I –

Charles   But you held on –

Dusabi   Hiding among the corpses of our friends, our neighbors, pushing away the rats –

Charles   But you lived –

Dusabi   Yes, and then one night they come –

Charles   The RPF –

Dusabi   Yes, the RPF finds us –

Charles   They find you –

Dusabi   They find me

And I open my eyes and let out a scream so they know we live

And the world becomes light, white –

Charles   White, light –

Dusabi   Elisabeth and I are saved.

Pause.

Charles   I saw it.

Dusabi   I know, Charles, I know.

Charles   Your body. Cut. Doused me in fuel. Wanting to burn you alive.

Dusabi   Yes.

Charles   And Elisabeth. Her hands

Dusabi   Cut to the bone. But she holds on.

Charles   The nun. Dusabi, she didn't come to help, did she? Sister Alice sang as the *interahamwe* slaughtered your friends and neighbors.

Shift. A cell.

Sister Justina   Forgive me Father, for I have sinned. It has been many days since my last confession.

She looks at the knife.

Her hand shakes.

She takes the knife in her hand.

Sister Justina   God, please grant me strength. The thoughts I have, Lord, take them from me. Let me live in your light, dear God.

And if I stray from your light, please find it in your heart to forgive me.

Blackout.

Day Four

Outside a home in Kigali.

Paul *eats, as* **Dusabi** *watches, his own food untouched.*

Paul   Eat, Dusabi.

Dusabi   Yes, yes.

Paul   There's news. The priest. Father Neromba. He was found. In Texas, America.

Should be tried here. But no. He will be tried with the nuns.

Dusabi   His capture. This is a good thing.

Paul   Is it? At first I thought so. But now. What if the court looks more favorably on the nuns in light of Father's crimes?

Dusabi   Do the nuns know?

Paul   Last night the older one, she tried to . . .

Pause. **Paul** *catches himself.*

Dusabi   What, Paul?

Paul   No, nothing.

It is not important. What is important is that the nuns will leave for Belgium sooner than expected. We got word last night. By the end of the weekend they'll be gone.

Dusabi   I will speak to them.

Paul   When I took Charles to the jail today, he was changed. Somehow. Changed.

Dusabi   We spoke about the church. Now. Finish your breakfast.

Paul   You sound like a father.

Dusabi   She gave me no children. God gave me you.

Paul   And why would God do that, eh?

Dusabi   He thinks I am not punished enough.

Dusabi *and* **Paul** *laugh.*

Dusabi   I feel quiet in my head. Today could be a good day.

Paul   Talking to Charles helped, no?

Dusabi   He made me a promise.

Paul   Not sure you should believe the promise of any American reporter.

Look. Haven't touched your breakfast. You should eat. You never eat.

Dusabi   Yes, look, look, Paul, I eat. I eat too.

Paul (*smiles*)

They eat.

Shift. An interrogation cell at the jail.

Sister Alice   Charles, why do you keep asking this question –?

Charles   It is a simple question, Sister.

Sister Alice   The men might have asked for supplies.

Charles   I asked about fuel, not supplies, not food. Fuel.

The RPF charge that you gave gasoline to the men. Captured *interahamwe* are on record, they've testified that the fuel used in these murders came from the rectory. That it was given freely. And that you knew what it was for.

Sister Alice   One of the men said his truck, that it needed –

Charles   You saw them murder a child. Why would you believe that?

Sister Alice   I did not give them fuel.

Charles   They burned people alive.

Sister Alice   I thought we had an arrangement.

Charles Arrangement?

Sister Alice No, I do not speak correctly. I mean an understanding. That you understand me.

I tried to help the Tutsis. Remember?

Charles I don't think you did.

Pause. **Sister Alice** *is shocked.*

Sister Alice Charles, do you think I would lie to you about such a thing?

Charles *looks at* **Sister Alice**.

Charles You wanted them wiped from the face of the earth
you saw it
their faces
the flames
charred flesh
meat dripping off bone
you did nothing
called out to you
called out
and you
you did nothing –

Sister Alice You were not here. You act like you know, but you do not know.

Charles It's as if you killed them with your own hands.

Sister Alice No! What Could I Do? What Could I Do? Refuse?

They did unspeakable things to women. I saw. I saw with my own eyes what they would do to me. You expect me to say to these men,

No I Will Not Give You Fuel.

They violate me, take the fuel regardless. Alive, alive, I could do something. And I did. I went into the church that night and gave assistance as best as I could.

You do not know. You were not here. Do not presume to judge me.

Charles   There is a survivor from the massacre.

Pause. **Sister Alice** *is shaken.*

Sister Alice   You know, there are no survivors. Someone is telling you stories. Playing with you. They will do anything to see us punished.

Charles   The massacre began when you were still at the church. And what did you do? You stood in the yard and sang to drown out the sound. Why didn't you help them?

Pause.

Sister Alice   I see I have made an error in confiding in you. Please tell the guard I am ready.

Charles   There was a situation last night. With Sister Justina.

Sister Alice   Bernadette. What has happened?

Charles   She hurt herself.

Sister Alice   There was an accident?

Charles   No. She hurt herself. Intentionally.

Sister Alice   I do not understand what you are saying.

Charles   She stole a knife and sharpened it.

She cut her wrist.

Sister Alice   Bernadette would not do that.

Charles   I'm sorry.

Sister Alice   She would never.

Charles   Can you tell me why she would do such a thing? Try and take her own life?

Sister Alice   I am done answering your questions.

Charles   I'll talk to the guards. Make sure they bring you to the infirmary so you can see her tonight. I know seeing you would help her.

Sister Alice   I do not understand you, Charles. You help me, you hurt me. I should learn by now. That is the way with men.

Shift. A hotel bar in Kigali.

Charles   I got angry. Angry at her. I kept seeing what happened in the church. Seeing it through Dusabi's eyes.

When I looked at Sister Alice, I couldn't help it.

Paul   You have the real story now, Charles. I am sure your editor Kendra will agree.

Charles   You have quite a memory, Paul.

Paul   She is your boss girlfriend.

Charles   Not sure she'd like that nickname.

Paul   The nun lied to you. Told you she took care of a child, helped Tutsis escape from the church. You cannot put her lies in your article. Think of what would happen to your reputation.

Pause.

Charles   How did you know that?

Paul   What do you mean, Charles?

Charles   I never told you what Sister Alice said to me.

Paul   Perhaps, Dusabi mentioned . . .

Charles   No.

Pause.

Charles   Everything in that jail is being recorded, isn't it?

Paul   I got you a better story. Maybe now you get to keep your job even after you steal another person's words.

Charles   What if what Sister Alice told me isn't a lie?

Paul   She helped no Tutsi.

Charles   What would make Justina try and take her life? That's a sin of the highest order.

Paul   What more of a sign of her guilt do you need?

Charles   There were hundreds and hundreds of people taking shelter there. If Alice did go in there and help a few escape, how would Dusabi even know?

Paul   After all you see, you refuse to believe what's in front of your face.

Charles   You think a nun would do that? Lie to me.

Paul   If you didn't believe that, you wouldn't have said what you said to her today.

Pause.

Charles   Nothing could change your mind. I have to be objective

Paul   I have seen men, women, priests, yes, nuns even, do far worse things than lie.

Charles   I like those mocha hoods, and I can't help / but think –

Paul   Hood? Hood? You are bad Catholic, Charles. That is a habit, not a hood. And I watched women in those habits hack babies clinging to their mother's back hack them to death all in the name of Hutu Power.

Charles   This place is fuckin' barbaric, Paul.

Paul   This coming from a man who lives in a country where everyone has guns. Men shooting children in the streets every day. You buy guns at the store like you buy potato. At least here Hutus do it with machete. They see up close what they do.

Charles   I've never killed anyone. Can you say that?

Paul   I'm a soldier.

Pause.

Charles   Did you find Dusabi and Elisabeth at the church?

Paul   They played dead for so long they almost become dead. But I looked at his face, saw him take a breath. I tell him I'm a friend and he opens his eyes.

Charles   For Elisabeth to live through such horror only to die in her sleep.

Paul   Is that what Dusabi tells you?

Charles   Did I misunderstand?

Paul   He is ashamed. We never speak of it.

Charles   What happened to Elisabeth?

Paul   Elisabeth kills herself, Charles. Uses his gun. He finds her.

Silence.

Charles   But Paul. She didn't . . .?

Paul   She didn't, what?

Charles   She didn't have hands. The militia –

Paul   I know. She uses her feet.

Pause.

Paul *laughs.*

Charles   Paul, stop –

Paul   Picture it –

Charles   Stop it –

Paul   She was a big woman –

Charles   Paul, how can you laugh?

Paul (*forceful*)   What do you want me to do? Cry? I cannot cry anymore, Charles. I laugh because it keeps me alive. I keep crying, then I should take my gun too and do the same

BOOM

Straight shot to the head and be done.

Charles   If God exists, he's a Bastard.

Paul   God is good. It is we who spoil this world.

Shift.

Charles (*to the recorder*)   What do I do? Tell truths, tell lies, tell what I know, or what I think I know. Tell the readers, our bosses, what they want to know to save my own skin. Maybe the problem is these categories – truth, lies – they just don't make sense anymore. Maybe they never did.

He shuts the recorder off.

Pause.

He turns it back on.

Charles (*into the recorder*)   You were my compass, Dan. You told me to listen, to watch, that if I paid attention, the truth would reveal itself. Told me to not get in the way of letting the facts reveal themselves. But I don't know if I know how to do that anymore.

Shift. A holding cell in the jail.

Sister Justina   It was an accident –

Sister Alice   He said, the reporter, he said –

Sister Justina   No, Consolata, it was dark. I couldn't see.
They had finally brought me some food. I was only trying to
cut corn –

Sister Alice   That's what I told him. She would never.

Sister Justina   You spoke with him again?

Sister Alice   Yes. All he asked was the fuel.

Sister Justina   What did you say?

Sister Alice   Something has come over him today. Before
he looked at me with gentle eyes, but today he would
not listen.

He looked disgusting like Tutsi.

Sister Justina   Consolata, do not speak like that.

Sister Alice   The story was to change the way we are looked
at. Now, it could damage us.

Sister Justina   What has become of us, plotting and
scheming? That is not who we are.

Sister Alice   I want us to return home. Do you not want
the same?

Sister Justina   I want to keep His laws.

Sister Alice   I ask again. Was it an accident?

Sister Justina   Yes.

Sister Alice   I told the reporter about a boy. Vincent.

Sister Justina   Vincent?

Sister Alice   How I watched him be murdered the night
before we were moved away.

Sister Justina   Consolata, I don't understand.

Sister Alice   I told him we sneak Tutsis from the church.

Sister Justina   What Have You Done?

Sister Alice   We are guilty of nothing.

Sister Justina   We made a vow to God to obey his commandments and you –

Sister Alice   I ask you a third time, Bernadette, was it an accident?

Sister Justina   Yes.

Sister Alice   You stand before me and you cannot speak the truth to my face. It was no accident. And yet you judge me for my sins.

Sister Justina   I picture it, when I close my eyes, the burning, the screams –

Sister Alice   We Kill No Tutsis. Why Must We Pay For Men's Sins?

Sister Justina   But we were there. We could've done something. Refuse to give the men fuel –

Sister Alice   I am Hutu. Tutsis kept us slaves for centuries. Father was right. Rwanda is a better place with less *inyenzi*.

Sister Justina   No.

Sister Alice   You agreed with Father.

Sister Justina   No. I always say Father was too easily swayed by power of those men –

Sister Alice   You never spoke against him when he proclaimed the evil of the *inyenzi*.

Sister Justina   What could I say to change the course of his thinking?

Sister Alice   Because inside we did believe what Father said. What Seth said. We might not have spoken it aloud but –

Sister Justina   No No This is not true –

Sister Alice   Bernadette, you believe in the evil of the *inyenzi*, do not pretend –

Sister Justina *raises her hand to strike* **Sister Alice**. **Sister Alice** *grabs her wrist.* **Sister Justina** *cries out in pain.*

Sister Alice   The wrong committed was not joining them in their work.

Sister Justina   Some evil has fallen on you. It is the men of the prison, they fill, fill your head with these thoughts. That's what this is.

Resist them.

Sister Alice   My only sin was not killing Tutsi when I could

I should have picked up machete

I should have given the men more fuel to burn more Tutsi

I want to smash them / grind them into the earth like cockroaches

Sister Justina   May God Burn The Tongue From Your Mouth

Sister Alice   Bernadette, I speak what you feel, inside. We will be punished as killers, why did we not cut and kill those who spit at us now?

Sister Justina   Because that is not who we are.

Sister Alice   In this world I cannot be who I was.

Blackout.

Day Five

An interrogation room at the jail.

Sound: church bells ring in the distance.

Sister Justina *does not look at* **Dusabi** *or* **Charles**.

Charles   Thank you for seeing me.

Sister Justina   They tell us we leave tonight.

Charles   There's been some developments. Because of Father Neromba's capture, the Belgians have moved the date of the trial.

Will Sister Alice join us –?

Sister Justina   No.

Charles   She refuses to speak to me?

Sister Justina   I am afraid, yes.

Pause. **Sister Justina** *locks eyes with* **Dusabi**.

Charles   Sister, this is Dusabi. He would like to speak with / you about –

Dusabi   I would like to speak to Sister alone, Charles.

Charles   Dusabi, I can't, I can't do that. We agreed –

Sister Justina   It is all right, Charles. You can go.

Silence.

Charles   I'll be right outside.

Charles *leaves.*

Dusabi   Sister, you are hurt.

Sister Justina   Sister Alice and I should be at Easter services, working with the children, celebrating. No, instead, we are here. And tonight, we will be taken away, maybe never to return.

Dusabi   We came to your church. My wife and I.

Pause. **Sister Justina** *is surprised, but tries to recover.*

Sister Justina   Those days those days feel so far away.

Dusabi   Not to me.

Sister Justina   You are not familiar to me. So many faces –

Dusabi   I thought I saw you with my own eyes, I would recognize you –

Sister Justina   All a blur in my mind.

Dusabi   My wife and I, we are the only survivors of what happened in your church.

Sister Justina   It was a holy place, a place of happiness and now –

Dusabi   My wife took her life last year.

Sister Justina   I am sorry.

Dusabi   Your wrist?

Sister Justina   A stupid accident. That is all.

Dusabi   Do not lie, Sister.

Sister Justina   I am weak.

Dusabi   The genocide, it continues.

Sister Justina   We are not guilty of any crime, I refuse –

Dusabi *goes to strike her. But he stops. They stare deeply into each other's eyes.*

Sister Justina   If you wish to strike me, do so. But know you cannot punish me more than I punish myself.

Silence.

This section should develop a cadence. They are almost speaking to themselves but find a point of connection by the end.

Dusabi   Why did you not help us?

Sister Justina   I I could do nothing, Dusabi –

Dusabi   The men cut me poured fuel over me –

Sister Justina   I gave them fuel yes I gave them fuel I had no choice –

Dusabi   My wife's arms were cut to the bone –

Sister Justina   I was scared they would hurt me take me rape me –

Dusabi   Came to me and for some reason did not finish the job –

Sister Justina   I heard them heard them say –

Dusabi   Prayed to God please let it end –

Sister Justina   We will kill the *inyenzi* –

Dusabi   Begged God to take this cross from me –

Sister Justina   I did not know what to do –

Dusabi   God, the weight of this thing is crushing me –

Sister Justina   Fear held me in the rectory –

Dusabi   We lay there like the dead –

Sister Justina   All I could do is pray –

Dusabi   You could have helped us –

Sister Justina   I could have helped you, tried –

Dusabi   Now when I close my eyes

Sister Justina and Dusabi   The things I see

Sister Justina   Forgive me, Dusabi

Forgive me please.

Sister Justina *is crying.*

Dusabi *takes her hand gently in his.*

Dusabi *begins to weep uncontrollably.*

Dusabi   I I I . . .

Dusabi *cannot finish the statement.*

Charles *enters.*

Sister Justina *cradles* **Dusabi**.

He watches for a moment.

Charles   I I I'm sorry.

They're asking questions, Dusabi.

Sister, the guard is waiting for you outside.

Sister Justina *looks at them both.*

Sister Justina   Goodbye, Dusabi.

Charles.

Charles *exits with* **Sister Justina**.

Dusabi *clutches his stomach. He doubles over in pain, gagging.*
Charles *enters.*

Charles   Dusabi –

Dusabi   Turn away –

Do not want you –

To see me –

Charles   Let me help you.

Charles *helps* **Dusabi** *stand.*

Dusabi   My light –

Charles   Dusabi, you will be all right –

Dusabi, Dusabi, listen to me –

Deep breath, deep breath, OK –?

Hold my hand

Dusabi *takes* **Charles**'s *hand.*

Charles   Tight

Tighter

I'll

I'll

Tell you a joke

OK

OK

OK.

What do lawyers do when they die?

Dusabi   Yes, tell me

Charles   No, you say, you say, I don't know

Dusabi   Again

Charles   What do lawyers do when they die?

Dusabi   I do not know

Charles   They lie still.

Charles *laughs. After a beat,* **Dusabi** *laughs too.*

Charles   You get it?

Dusabi   No.

Charles   It's, ah, a play on lie, like in don't tell the truth, and lie, like lay down.

Dusabi   No I see that. Why is that funny?

Charles   C'mon!

Dusabi   Paul is right. You are not funny.

The two men smile at each other. **Dusabi** *embraces him closely.*

Silence.

Dusabi   I forgive her, Charles.

Shift. The yard in front of the church.

Paul   You keep your promise.

Charles   The guards dropped me off.

Paul   I hear you are leaving.

Charles   With the nuns headed to Belgium, I leave tonight.

Paul   You have a story to finish.

Charles   Dusabi forgave her, Paul.

Paul   That is not something I understand.

Charles   I need to go inside the church before I go. To write this story. I have to.

But. I'm scared. Not just a photograph. Not just a picture in my mind. It will be there, right in front of me.

Paul   We left the bodies as we found them.

You will see

A child's skull cracked in two

A wrist reaching out to clutch another's

Charles   Dusabi and Elisabeth lying among those bodies

Hoping to be safe

Hoping it would stop

Those doors opening and –

Paul   You will never forget this.

Charles   Paul, I'm ready.

The sound of the nuns singing, somewhere in the space. The singing grows louder and louder until it becomes deafening.

Sisters Justina and Alice
Jesus loves me
This I know
Because the Bible tells me so
Little ones to Him belong
For they are weak

But He is Strong
Yes, Jesus / Loves Me
Yes, Jesus Loves Me
Yes, Jesus Loves Me
The Bible tells me so
Jesus loves me
This I know
As He loved so long ago
Taking children on his knee
Saying
Let them come to me
Yes, Jesus Loves Me . . .

As the nuns sing . . .

Charles   We walk toward the church
the door opens
and I hear singing, impossible singing
like the singing Dusabi heard that night
it grows louder and louder
the voices of the nuns
multiplying, distorting in the evening sky
we stand inside of the church
the blinding light of annihilation and hope
of past and future
of death and life
of pain and the drug that banishes all grief
of a truth
that burns and burns
the darkness
forever and ever
and ever
and ever
and

A blinding blinding light.

Blackout.

End of play.

Pronunciation Guide

Habyrarimana [Hey-bay-air-e-man-ahh]: the surname of the third Rwandan President.

Interahamwe [In-air-ahm-way]: the Hutu Power militias responsible for organizing and carrying out the killings. The 'way' sound is not strongly pronounced. A native speaker would make it sound more like 'in-air-ahm.' Charles pronounces the 'way.'

Inyenzi [In-yen-zee]: 'Cockroach,' a derogatory term for the Tutsi used by the Hutu Power movement. The 'yen' is spoken just like the word for the Japanese currency. The 'z' is like the 's' in 'please.'

Muhere aruhande [Moo-hair-eh Ah-roo-hahn-deh]: 'Go about the task systematically from one place to another.' The final 'eh' vowel sound is pronounced.

Mana, wari uri he? [Mahn-ah, war-ee ooh-ree hay?]: 'God, where were you?' Blend 'uri he' as if one word 'ooh-ree-hay.' Lead up to the end, as you would a question in English.

In the London production, the song 'Jesus Loves Me' was sung by Kinyarwandan. The phonetic arrangement for that production was:

Yesu arankunda
Ibi ndabizi
Kuko na Bibibiliya ariko ivuga ngo abana bato ni abe kuko ari
abanyantege nke
Ariko we ni umyambaraga (umunyangufu)
Yego Yesu arankunda
Yesu arankunda yego
Yesu arankunda Bibiliya niko imbwira
Yesu arankunda
Ibi ndabizi
Nuko na mbere yakikiye abana
Numureke basange
Yesu arankunda

9 781474 248495